Can I Offer You A Cigarette?

The only sure way to break the smoking habit!

Stephen A. Berkeley

Copyrights & Digital License

Publisher:
CM BERKELEY MEDIA GROUP
Ontario, Canada
First Edition

Digital ISBN: 978-0-9811493-1-8
Print ISBN: 978-1-989612-33-0

Digital Edition License Notes

Stephen A. Berkeley

Acknowledgements

There are a few people I'd like to thank.

First of all, I'd like to give thanks to God. His influence in my life has helped me to be positive in the presence of life's trials. I'd like to thank my publisher for working with me and holding my hand through the process of publishing my book. This is a very personal story and one which I am honoured to share.

To all the others whose names are not mentioned here but who have touched my life with their love and their kindness. You're a part of my writing this book.

I dedicate this book to my lovely daughter Sarah who continues to be my motivation to want to be more than I am.

* * * * *

About This Edition

Publisher's Note:

This book was originally released as a strictly digital edition back in 2010 when e-books were still something on the fringe or rather the bleeding edge of books.

As we're approaching the 10th anniversary of this short read, we re-releasing it on Kindle and other popular e-reader plus we're doing a print edition! It's the same great book but we've updated the publisher materials, and added in some questions at the end of the chapter since this format works in the print edition where you can write in the book. You might see references to TV advertising of tobacco products which hasn't been available in years.

Oh, and Stephen was the recipient of an award from the President of the United States for excellence in volunteerism. We included the images on the following page. Enjoy this classic book.

* * * * *

Stephen A. Berkeley

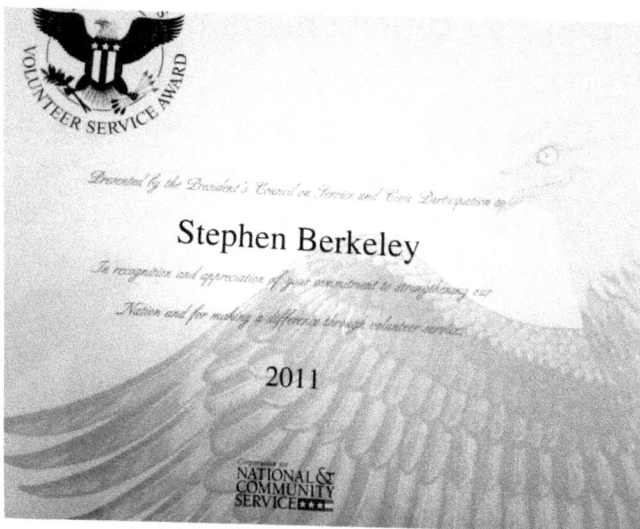

VOLUNTEER SERVICE AWARD

Presented by the President's Council on Service and Civic Participation to

Stephen Berkeley

In recognition and appreciation of your commitment to strengthening our Nation and for making a difference through volunteer service.

2011

CORPORATION FOR
NATIONAL &
COMMUNITY
SERVICE ★★★

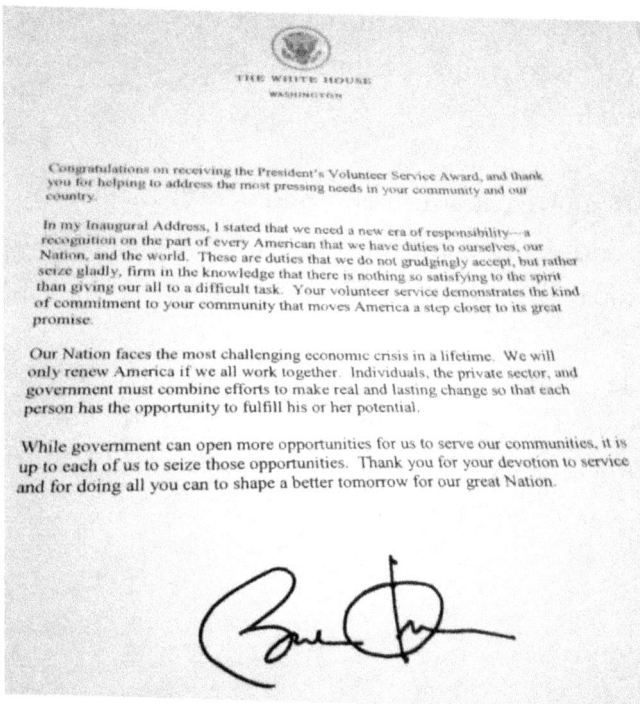

THE WHITE HOUSE
WASHINGTON

Congratulations on receiving the President's Volunteer Service Award, and thank you for helping to address the most pressing needs in your community and our country.

In my Inaugural Address, I stated that we need a new era of responsibility—a recognition on the part of every American that we have duties to ourselves, our Nation, and the world. These are duties that we do not grudgingly accept, but rather seize gladly, firm in the knowledge that there is nothing so satisfying to the spirit than giving our all to a difficult task. Your volunteer service demonstrates the kind of commitment to your community that moves America a step closer to its great promise.

Our Nation faces the most challenging economic crisis in a lifetime. We will only renew America if we all work together. Individuals, the private sector, and government must combine efforts to make real and lasting change so that each person has the opportunity to fulfill his or her potential.

While government can open more opportunities for us to serve our communities, it is up to each of us to seize those opportunities. Thank you for your devotion to service and for doing all you can to shape a better tomorrow for our great Nation.

About This Book

This book is based on the real life experience of a man who smoked for twenty-two years, but who took a conscious decision to quit. It compels the reader to take a long look inside, and make a decision about his life, for good or bad.

Ultimately, it is about the true test of one's will, and begs the question, do you have what it take to be the true master of your will? God's will is for you to live a healthy and disease-free life, but your poorly exercised and ultimately destructive will, is to embrace habits which destroy your body.

If you've read this book, and believe that you are serious about improving your complete self, then today is your day to quit smoking for good.

The author concludes, that God can only help you, if you are willing to co-operate with him, in the process of re-imposing your control (WILL) over all situations in your life.

* * * * *

Stephen A. Berkeley

Foreword

Writing a foreword to a book about quitting smoking is something of a new experience for me. I have never smoked and found the habit to be somewhat unpleasant to my senses.

Having read this book, however, I can say that smoking is a metaphor for all aspects of your life. In every aspect of your life you and others are struggling for control. That may be control over sleeping too much, control over being late, control over negative thoughts and emotions, or anything else that is not beneficial to your life. What Stephen has done is take his very personal journey in the process of kicking the smoking habit, and told it for you, the reader, to appreciate how much God can help you to overcome smoking.

In seeing and understanding his journey, you can begin to look at other areas where you need the victory over what holds you in bondage. This little book is a wonderful resource for Christians and non-Christian who desire to know God's help to overcome smoking and then move on to greater challenges. If you think God has not worked for you in the past, you can reconsider giving Him another chance after reading this book.

I know that believers will find something to take away from Stephen's journey. I encourage you to get this book and encourage others to get it and quit smoking.

Vaughn Berkeley, MBA

Author of The Break The Poverty Curse: Unlock Your Prosperity Book Series.

* * * * *

Stephen A. Berkeley

Contents

Knowing How It All Began

Chapter 1

* * *

"Looking back on your past can help you create a better future." ~ Vaughn Berkeley

"Behold, I come quickly. My reward is with me…" ~ Revelation 22:12

* * *

"I tried quitting so many times, but I just don't seem to be able to do it, I just CAN"T."

How many times have you said that to yourself?

Smoking is a habit you developed, and to become the habitual smoker that you have become, you practiced smoking. Do you remember the very first time you drew in that lung-full of smoke? Ooh, you coughed so hard, your eyes watered, your throat hurt, you thought you would die.

Remember what you said then, " this is not for me, I'm never going to smoke again".

The problem is, that the considerable peer pressure from your friends far out-weighed the discomfort of your shocked lungs. So here you are today, a seasoned smoker, who, having taken stock of things would like to stop, even wishing secretly that you had never started in the first place.

Well, if you accept my help, together, with God's guidance, we are a formidable team. Having realized that your efforts to quit were unsuccessful so far, you must know that you need help. In my situation, I found this affirmation to be very profound, " I can do all things through Christ which strengthens me, " (Philippians 4:13).

The moment you understand that you have access to another source of strength, to help you meet this challenge, your whole mind-set is renewed. We can attack and defeat one of the smallest, but most dangerous of enemies you ever had to face.

The great news is that you have already been

declared the winner, because you made the right choice. You were born a winner, so there are no limits to what you can achieve, and breaking this addiction should be a done deal. The only one who could prevent you is your will - what do you want?

Unwittingly, you were enticed to give this enemy absolute permission to take up residence in your body, and he took full advantage of it. Now, having made the decision to quit, we are going to terminate his lease, toss him out unceremoniously, and retake control.

Over and above everything else, YOU must take control, no one can do it for you. There is going to be a restoration cost, for his tenancy has resulted in some structural damage. Like a very bad tenant, he messed-up the house, and left without throwing out the garbage. So now, repairs are going to be necessary after you evict this tenant, and you have to do the clean-up yourself.

I used to be a smoker, but I quit TWENTY-TWO years ago. Having smoked for sixteen years, I had got to the point of smoking a stunning five to six packs of cigarettes a day. Thankfully, I was honest enough to admit to myself that my smoking was not a way to "ease my pressures" or "to calm my nerves" or any number of excuses smokers use to justify continuing this destructive habit.

I remember when I was a high school principal, one day it was reported to me that a female student was smoking in the bathroom. Realizing that she was discovered, she tried to put out the cigarette between her fingers, and I imagine she also tried to release the smoke in her mouth and lungs through some other unseen hole in her head. The only thing she did was almost burn her fingernails out, but her major problem was to get rid of the smoke that was gradually choking her to death, without us seeing it. At that point I told her that she could exhale and when she did she almost collapsed. This situation might have been funny, if not for the realization of the danger to which this very young girl had exposed herself.

Truth is, I had started smoking to identify with my friends - they smoked, so I started to smoke, and it seemed fashionable at the time. This girl was trying to impress her peers that she could

smoke in the bathroom and not get caught.
Unfortunately for her, she did get caught, and
that gave me the opportunity to work with a
young potential smoker pre-emotively to ensure
that this habit will not be practiced again.

As a matter of fact, this foolish habit I started got
me my first girlfriend, because she smoked
occasionally as well. I was also given the double
dare so I continued smoking from then until I
got to the point of knowing that I wanted to quit.

The first step to quitting is QUITTING!

The healing process requires that you speak to
yourself the reason why you started to smoke in
the first place. When you know the cause, you
can effectively identify and deal with the effect.
Any bad habit that you joined yourself to, will
not be broken without you as the central and
controlling shareholder. Your WILL is the gate
you alone must unlock to finally free yourself of
this habit, and walk away in victory.

As time passed, I became more and more
conscious about the habit, and noted secretly to
myself the changes taking place in my own body.

Also, I sweated profusely, and in spite of the expensive colognes I always liked and used, strangely enough, I was always conscious of the ever present burnt tobacco smell on my clothes and body. These aspects of smoking are never glorified in the tobacco ads bombarding the airwaves and billboards. The idea is to create a deep sense of denial whenever confrontations about the ill-effects of smoking arise.

For me, the house never smelled quite right, though I would never admit this to myself, or anyone else for that matter.

The most unfortunate thing about my smoking was that I was very conscious of the wrongness of the habit. I knew as well that I would have to deal with the consequences if I did not quit, yet, I chose to continue. At one time, my son, whom I loved dearly, told me that I was "polluting his space." Although it hurt to hear this from him, I believe he loved me enough to enumerate the dangers of smoking, even the possibility of developing cancer, yet, I was not ready to quit.

Smokers tend to develop a persecution complex against people who talk to them about quitting, and one time I jokingly told my son that I believed that he was being paid to direct "stop smoking" advertisements at me. You must believe me when I say, that this place of denial is a cold and lonely place.

Becoming defensive will not promote honest soul searching, and only serves to entrench the habit. The enemies of doubt and discouragement will not surrender, so it is imperative that you work at it. Practice does not make perfect, as the old adage tells us, it makes permanent, only what you practice you become good at.

* * * * *

Chapter Summary

In this chapter, we see learned that you have to confront the smoking demon head on. You have been in bondage and with God's help, you can take those steps to become free.

Chapter Exercise

1) Why did you start smoking?

_____

_____

_____

2) What motivated to keep doing it after you first felt it was wrong?

_____

_____

_____

3) Why do you want to quit now?

_____

_____

_____

* * * * *

The Control Factor
Chapter 2

* * *

"Are you really in control? Control brings worry and anxiety about losing control." ~ Vaughn Berkeley

"Which of you, by being anxious, can add one moment to his lifespan?" (Matthew 6:27)

* * *

Even though my act of quitting did not include economic considerations as a deterrent, the actual cost to me in terms of dental among other things, should have sounded the alarms. Still, I did not take the decision to engage in self-actualization of my sovereignty and take control of this habit.

No one will accuse you of unfair advantage if you get on the bully platform against this smaller yet very influential and controlling foe. Several times, when I talk to people about quitting smoking, they say to me, "I will quit sometime soon", and I remarked to a young lady recently, that I pray for her sake that her quitting is not preceded by death, she was chain-smoking so hard I became alarmed for her.

Over the years, I have observed the demeaning things that people do when the nicotine in the bloodstream called out for another " fix ". In my time of smoking, if for some reason I found myself without a cigarette late in the night hours, I remember taking up the spent butts from the ashtray, unfolding them and lighting them. Friends, even that most disgusting taste of old hardened nicotine was not sufficient to scream STOP!

It is an addiction and a curse, and you must see it for what it is. There were times when I actually went out into the street in the very late hours of the night to see if there was someone on the street at that hour, from whom I could solicit a nicotine fix. When the poison in your bloodstream calls out like a baby cries out for a bottle, the smoker feels compelled to supply that need - a cigarette.

For as long as I could remember, I have heard so

many excuses why people smoke, from a broken relationship to very bad news, to being nervous, to feeling cold, to just wanting to relax, the list is unending. Speaking from my own experience as well, I have difficulty understanding why anyone would wish to add the prospect of an early and sometimes very painful death, or health complications, to the problems they can scarcely cope with.

The truth of the matter is that studies have shown that cigarette manufacturers increased by 11%, the volume of nicotine per cigarette a smoker inhales. This make the addiction much more difficult to break, and it guarantees a lifetime market from those who have not made a conscious decision to quit. This calls for a tag team effort - your WILL coupled with God's strength, an unassailable combination. Because the demon of smoking never hesitates to entrench itself whenever the opportunity arises, smoking is not a habit you TRY to break, it's something you QUIT.

God will not act against your will - you must be a willing participant. He will help you if you ask for his help.

Stephen A. Berkeley

At the time of tobacco addiction, the smoker does not see it as a bad habit, rather, he merely see it as choosing between "smoking or non-smoking sections" when asked. This is part of the battery of lies that the devil whispers to convince smokers to stay with the habit. In reality, the reason most people remain trapped in this addiction is simply a lack of self control and assertiveness.

I always say, if I could do it (quit), anyone can. There is a power so much greater than you and I just lying there deep within us, waiting for us to embrace it, and it feels good when we express this power. The fact is, the more we exercise this power, the stronger we become, and the more empowered we feel when we reject the desire to have a smoke.

In my early twenties, having already become a seasoned smoker, I remember telling myself that I am the one who adopted this abominable habit, and I will never demean myself further, by asking someone else for a cigarette. As a result, I started to purchase cigarettes by the cartons instead of by individual packs. This naturally gave me a false feeling of being a superior smoker, since it would be unlikely that I would run out, and be tempted to beg for a cigarette. There is no such thing as a superior smoker. The demon assigned to keep you smoking plays on the human's natural inclination to be superior to someone else. The lies continue.

Needless to say, all this did, was to make me into a larger consumer of nicotine, and my habit fed itself, creating a need to smoke ever increasing amounts, because of the ease of accessibility. Something else started happening as well, other "low level" smokers stopped buying cigarettes, and started feeding off me, which fact was not lost on me. For me, I felt the righteous indignation of the reasoned mind that intoned, that I was the one who embraced my habit, therefore I must support its financial requirements. Naturally I felt that in a similar way, everybody should buy their own (cigarettes) death, and I must not be responsible for anyone else' habit.

You would think that after such exceptional reasoning I would have dropped the habit like a hot potato. Alas no, because the nature of an addiction is to defy all logic, and it will only relinquish its hold when an iron will is asserted forcefully against it.

At the time of what I consider one of the greatest tragedies of life, an irreparably broken marriage, I took a very hard look at myself and made an honest confession to myself. I realized that I did not like myself very much, and herein lies one of the cruellest motivations that control the human tragedy of tobacco addiction. Very often, we create reasons to celebrate smoking one, for example, the boss yells at you, "I need a smoke", you disagree with your spouse, "I need a smoke", you get some bad news, " I need a smoke". Notice the emphasis is NOT on finding a solution to whatever the problem is, but on "I NEED A SMOKE!"

It is a most powerful message to receive and understand, when we can know that "I" am in control, therefore, instead, I will say, "I" am in control, " I do not need a smoke". Your greatest strength is in saying it. The very essence of control impacts on the fact that God gave us humans, the greatest weapon that we can ever use, and that is a will.

Even though parents tend to frown on a strong-willed child, especially one who is intent on individual thought and action, there are extreme benefits to be derived from constantly exercising one's will.

Fortunately for me, during my years of smoking, talking to God always allowed me to turn disappointment into a positive step towards better self control. Do not shift the blame, take responsibility for starting the habit in the first place. It puts the healing process to work in earnest, with no room for denials.

* * * * *

Chapter Summary

In this chapter we discussed a key point about how smoking seems to give you control of the situation. This is fake of course but in the moment, it distracts you from the pressures of the moment. We talked about regaining control.

Chapter Exercise

1) What are some moments when you feel the need to grab a cigarette to regain some "control"?

_____

_____

_____

2) Instead of running for a cigarette, what are some other ideas to face the situation?:

_____

_____

_____

* * * * *

Identify and Break the Stronghold

Chapter 3

* * *

"Strongholds are good for owner of them but terrible for those attempting to break it down." ~ Vaughn Berkeley

"No weapon that is formed against you will prevail; and you will condemn every tongue that rises against you in judgment..." (Isaiah 54:17)

* * *

Many times over the years, I have said to my students, when you recognize that you have reached the bottom of the barrel, you should rejoice, because you cannot fall any further.

The only way for you is UP!

As a matter of fact, quite recently, one of the

most challenging students I had years ago, and whom I have come to embrace as one of my own children, reminded me of my words, and how it often helped her overcome challenges in her life. This also applies to that point where you make a life-changing decision, especially if it is literally a gut-wrenching one. I guarantee that it will only get better, because you made the decision - you exercised your will.

During my early years as a public servant, I worked with a senior officer who would invariably ask me for a cigarette every morning as a ritual.

Unfortunately, that ritual set the pattern for the day, as he would seek one as often as he felt like it. He was a man many years my senior, and there was a similarly very large chasm between his salary and mine.

Logically, one would think that I should probably have been the one to ask him for a cigarette instead, although, I never ever did ask. Being a practical person, I must admit that he helped inform my decision to start buying my death by the cartons as previously stated. There was this day when he asked me for a cigarette, and instead of giving him one, I offered him a whole pack. He became very angry, as he suggested that my subtle message to him was, take the whole pack and consider it my dismissive gift, DON"T ASK AGAIN!

Naturally, this started a rather eloquent discourse between us as I used well-versed semantics to convince him that I was giving out of my abundance. Very cunningly at the same time, I took the opportunity to let him know that I bought cigarettes by the cartons. His response was then, and remains unprintable, even though he has been dead these last twelve years, due to self-promoted coronary disease.

The addiction to nicotine finds a natural ally in caffeine, and during my smoking years, I found them inseparable. In fact, I remember traveling to South America on several business trips, and one of the things that I made a habit of bringing back was coffee, some of the strongest I had ever tasted.

This habit (caffeine) could hold no attraction for me after quitting smoking. For me, the moment

I lost the desire for one, the other addiction had no purpose for existence in me, so I quit drinking coffee almost at the same time that I quit smoking.

My will was exercised, and I can SAY literally, I HAVE SPOKEN !   First of all, I had to make the decision to quit smoking, and the decision to quit the coffee made itself, because I recognized the connection.

Whatever the message you send to the brain, good or bad, that is what it processes, and instructs the rest of the body to fall in line with that decision. This process is the same for everybody, because it is a very personal decision that each individual must make after honest and sincere self evaluation. It is your will that you exercise, and therefore it does not depend on what anybody else thinks.

There is no need for a crutch to lean on when you are sufficiently convinced that **your will is superior to any suggestion** that the addiction may offer. It is not a very good idea to take up a substitute bad habit to replace smoking, like sucking mints for example, as that prevents you from realizing the full benefit of your decision to quit.

Having made a self-evaluation, the next step is to decide the importance of maintaining healthy habits, and eliminating those things which have a strong pulling power back to the addiction. I remember having a bad dream many years after I quit, and in that dream I found myself smoking again, and immediately I felt like I had betrayed my best friend - ME. The result was that I awoke in a state of shock and found myself deeply upset that I had been conquered by a foe I had already defeated.

This is evidence of the commitment that I had made to myself. The will I exercised was something that I lived, and it was real. **I said it aloud to myself so that I can identify how serious I was about the decision.** That is the staying power and fortitude of a strong will, against any foe. The most effective commitment that you will ever make is to do it for you, because you decided - it's your decision - it's your will.

From a health perspective, years of bombarding your lungs and your bloodstream with smoke and nicotine would have created certain strongholds in you. Consequently, it would therefore require "strong will" to defeat something that already has a "strong-hold".

Additionally, you become more susceptible to heart attacks or strokes, because the excessive tar left in your bloodstream will seek refuge in your arteries just like bad cholesterol does, and will do the much damage. If for no other reason, this should be a strong incentive to any serious-minded person to quit or never start if you do not smoke. The unfortunate truth is, that these are not considerations which shape the decision to start smoking or not. The decision to quit smoking should accompany a desire to pursue healthier eating and living standards, if you exercise your will to improve self.

When a last will and testament is written, the intention of the person leaving such a document is that these final wishes supersede whatever anyone else may desire. It is legally binding, and established right of presence and ownership to determine how disposal is effected.

Having exercised your will to quit smoking, that

should be the over-riding consideration which informs how you live after that.

* * * * *

Chapter Summary

In this chapter we looked at the power of the will and the need for you to vocally express it in order to actualize it.

Chapter Exercise

1) When you feel doubts and fears of falling back into that bad habit, what sentence could you vocalize? Write it below.

_____

_____

_____

2) Every morning when you wake up, what is the message that you could affirm to yourself in the mirror? Write it below.

_____

_____

_____

* * * * *

I Win - I Offered Myself A Cigarette

Chapter 4

* * *

"You win or lose by the way you choose." ~ Vaughn Berkeley

"I call heaven and earth to witness against you today, that I have set before you life and death, the blessing and the curse. Therefore choose life, that you may live, you and your descendants;" ~ Deuteronomy 13:19

* * *

As everything else in life, there are consequences that follow any life altering decisions that an individual chooses to make. In Luke 15:18 the moment the prodigal son says " I WILL ARISE", (a life altering decision), he took control, there were no opposing forces within him capable of preventing him from rising to a higher level. When you impose your will on that addiction, there is nothing to hinder your decision to quit smoking.

Truthfully, the price demanded for re-establishing your control is not outside your ability to cope with. Here, the expression no pain - no gain is not a cliché, but something that applies itself literally to the situation. My experience quitting smoking, has not been without its share of pain. The fact is, in the same way that I made a conscious decision to quit, I had to understand that I had a stronghold and that it required a stronger power to rid myself of its grip.

The time I chose to quit, was a time of deep crisis, and therefore, when the victory was won, I savoured it, and it was more meaningful, because I affirmed my will power against all odds.

Satan used every means at his disposal to draw me back to smoking, especially because at this time, I felt my spirit broken to the point where I felt drained. I made another critical assessment of my life, and concluded that I still felt very unhappy with myself and where I was heading.

I remember starting to pray earnestly, and found myself praying and desiring to quit any habits that are against my well-being. Through force of habit, I reached for a cigarette, and simultaneously started coughing - a nasty unproductive cough, so that I remember that I didn't smoke anymore. This went on for a while, my eyes were watering, and when I finally coughed something up that I could spit out, the relief was short-lived. But, God made a way of escape for me.

Lying flat on my back, looking up at the ceiling, I was beginning to get a different perspective of life. I needed a smoke very badly, or so the little demon tried to convince me, but the way I coughed, it just didn't feel good. I found myself asking God to help me to stop wanting to smoke.

Somehow, it seemed to me that everything will be ok as long as I could NOT want to smoke. In the midst of all of this, I had the nagging feeling deep down in the pit of my stomach that it was very easy to quit, if only I can find the resolve to shake the desire. I heard myself asking God to take away the desire for tobacco, and I don't care if it kills me, I will never smoke again.

Those words that I spoke were sincere words, and it was as if something was welling up in me.

Do not ask God to talk to you or do something in you, if you are not ready to hear him speak, or see him work.

It was on that fateful day that God himself gave me the only recipe to quit smoking forever. He said, "I already put the remedy inside you before you were born, all you have to do is use the key to access it." I felt confused, and the first thought I had after that was that the key, whatever it is, could not still work because I had polluted my body with these years of abusing tobacco.

Then God further told me that there is great power in the spoken word, he had formed the heaven and the earth by speaking the word, and as it is in heaven so it is on earth. His power is in us to accomplish things in the same way. In Philippians 2:13, the bible says "For it is God which works in you both to WILL and to do of his good pleasure."

God said to me, that if I spoke the words, and through my ears gate my brain heard those words, then they become the life to change anything. All I had to do was say aloud to myself so that I can hear myself, "Stephen, can I offer you a cigarette?" and I must answer myself so that my ears gate transmit the answer to my brain, "No thank you, I do not smoke anymore." There is a therapeutic salve released into the situation which causes the words to accomplish the result that you expect, but it only happens when you really believe it, and SAY IT!

From the very first time that you speak the words, and you answer the offer in the prescribed way, something changes - a power that says "I am in control, so I could say no," is released. You feel an inner strength when you refuse. It is like a concentrated shot of vitamin C when you feel the cold coming on. With every time that you feel to smoke a cigarette, and you speak to yourself, your stakes get higher, and each time, you get stronger.

Your will is being reinforced as you impose it on the situation. It is the ultimate reward that you can give yourself by turning the very thing, "the offer of a cigarette" against itself, "no thank you I do not smoke anymore" by co-opting its help to reject itself.

If you are at that point where you are ready to quit smoking, this is the only guaranteed way, and today is the best day to quit.

All that it requires is that you dig deep inside and find the key. You have heard "Just SAY no to drugs" etc, so why not "Just SAY no thank you I do not smoke anymore." Something good begins happening when you SAY it.

A good practice is to ask God constantly for his strength every time that you feel your will weakened, so you don't have to do it by yourself, so practice your victory like this:
Father, I ask for your help in this venture, let me speak with your voice so that I may truly hear, and that it may take effect on my life immediately, I accept the victory - I Quit -
(SAY YOUR NAME)   Can I offer you a cigarette?
Answer : No thank you, I do not smoke anymore.

Practice this every time you have an urge to smoke, and see and feel the surge of power in you every single time you reject the offer. Say it loudly to yourself and you must hear yourself boldly refuse the offer. The sense of victory is very satisfying, and will have a spin-off in other areas of your life.

* * * * *

Chapter Summary

In this chapter we looked at the process for gaining the victory. This step is important should the devil attempt to tempt you in the future.

Chapter Exercise

1) God is ready and willing to help you break free from your addiction. Pray and ask him to give you a word of encouragement. Write it below.

_____

_____

_____

2) Do you have a faithful friend who can help you? Write that person's name below and reach out to them.

_____

_____

_____

* * * * *

About The Author

Stephen A. Berkeley

Stephen Berkeley has been a High School Principal and Teacher, who enjoyed working with students from dysfunctional backgrounds. Today, these students would be called high risk students. This passion was evident in the results achieved by those students. Many of them after having been under his tutelage were able to pass their CXC and GCE exams. They subsequently went on to lead productive lives.

Stephen Berkeley was also an avid smoker having smoked for sixteen years. He had reached a rate of five to six packs each day.

Thankfully, he quit the habit cold turkey, and never returned to the habit. Being instructed by

God on the only way to quit, he has committed himself to helping others to break this addiction by simply applying the most powerful tool each of us possesses, YOUR Will.

In the last few years, he has been struggling and suffering with terrible back pain due to a spinal injury. Even with the prospect of facing unbearable pain daily, he still keeps a positive outlook tries to bring a smile and a bit of wisdom to those around him.

This book was written under trying circumstances but was made for you. It is his most sincere wish that this most compelling book will safely and surely instruct you on how to break this habit for good, as he has done for the past twenty-two years.

You can reach out to him via the publisher website.

* * * * *

More from CM Berkeley Media Group

CM Berkeley Media Group, based in Canada, works with its authors to produce books which help to uplift the human spirit, spread the message of health and wellness, and offer practical insights in finances, and other areas.

Website: cmberkeleymediagroup.com

Grab these other great titles at Amazon worldwide and other major online booksellers.

For Adults

- Break The Poverty Curse: Unlock Your Prosperity (2017 Edition)
- Break The Poverty Curse: Unlock Your Prosperity 2019 Success Planner
  (A Great tool for 10 to adults. Learn basic necessary life planning skills)
- Break The Poverty Curse: Unlock Your Prosperity 2019 Success Planner - ULTIMATE Edition
  (A Great tool for 17 to adults. This contains more information to help structure your progress)
- Break The Poverty Curse: Unlock Your Prosperity 2019 Success Planner - WRITER'S Edition
  (A great tool for 17 to adults who have dreams of becoming an author. Use this planner to write your book in under a year)
- Break The Poverty Curse: Unlock Your Prosperity - Puzzle Power 1
- Break The Poverty Curse: Unlock Your Prosperity - Puzzle Power 2
- Break The Poverty Curse: Unlock Your Prosperity - Puzzle Power 3

Stephen A. Berkeley

- Break The Poverty Curse: Unlock Your Prosperity 2020 Success Planner - ULTIMATE Edition
- Break The Poverty Curse: Unlock Your Prosperity 2020 Success Planner - School of Prophets Edition
- Break The Poverty Curse: Unlock Your Prosperity - CRASH PROOF
- Break The Poverty Curse: Unlock Your Prosperity (2020 Edition)

Jenny's 99 Health Quotes To Empower Your Life

Eating4Eternity: Unlock Your Holistic Health Lifestyle. Sweet Raw Desserts: Life Is Sweet Raw™

Can I Offer You A Cigarette: The Only Sure Way To Break The Smoking Habit

Colon By Design: Overcoming The Stigma Of Colon Sickness And Unlocking True Colon Health™

Fresh Food4Life™: The Case For Taking Back Control of Your Food And Empowering Your Family And Community.

For Teens and Young Adults
The Youth Leadership Empowerment System™

Jump into the world of Dr Vicktor Maximitas, world famous psychologist by day and legendary demon hunter by night. Go into this mystery world where good triumphs over evil and souls are rescued from demonic clutches. This is a new series by Vaughn Berkeley.
- A Maximitas Novel: Unholy Fyre (Book 1)
- A Maximitas Novel: Unholy Fyre (Book 2)
- A Maximitas Novel: Unholy Fyre (Book 3)

Can I Offer You A Cigarette

Coming in 2019/2020, Dr Max meets with Chastity and begins to piece together a puzzle of a dark and dangerous coven. Can he save the Chastity before time runs out?

- A Maximitas Novel: The DC74 File (Book 1)
- A Maximitas Novel: The DC74 File (Book 2)
- A Maximitas Novel: The DC74 File (Book 3)

For Children

The Adventures of Moshe Monkey and Elias Froggy book series.

- The Adventures of Moshe Monkey and Elias Froggy: A Healthy Business (Volume 1)
- Moshe and Elias Build A Garden (The Adventures of Moshe Monkey and Elias Froggy) (Volume 2)
- Moshe and Elias Tropical Vacation (The Adventures of Moshe Monkey and Elias Froggy) (Volume 3)
- Living Foods for Boys and Girls (The Adventures of Moshe Monkey and Elias Froggy) (Volume 4)
- Moshe Monkey Breaks His Leg (The Adventures of Moshe Monkey and Elias Froggy) (Volume 5)
- Moshe And Elias 2019 Daily Success Planner
- Moshe And Elias - Puzzle Book 1

Mouzzie Goes Home (Mouzzie Mouse Adventures) (Book 1)

* * * * *

Check out these titles on Amazon and major online book sellers.

Stephen A. Berkeley

Great Resources

Berkeley Family Art (berkeleyfamilyart.com)
This site showcases the original artwork by members of the Berkeley Family. You can order originals and prints from this site.

VaughnBerkeley.com
This is the website of Vaughn Berkeley. On there you'll see examples of Vaughn's writing style that leaves his fans raving. Vaughn also disciples others in the path of the early Christian church.

CM Berkeley Media Group (cmberkeleymediagroup.com)
This is the publisher website and it also contains information about a course to write your book in 90 days. If GOD has placed a message on your heart for the world, check out this site.

Eating4Eternity.org (www.eating4eternity.org)
Eating4Eternity is founded by Jenny Berkeley and is focused on her personal coaching approach. This member site is great for working with this godly woman of faith in health and wellness.

EternityWatch Magazine (eternitywatchmagazine.com)
EternityWatch Magazine is the premier magazine for those seeking a truly holistic approach to health and wellness.

Berkeley Academy (http://berkeley.academy)
This is the online educational institute founded by Vaughn Berkeley and carrying on the tradition and heritage of the Berkeley name and role in educating the masses. Vaughn's passion has been education from as long as he can remember.

* * * * *

www.ingramcontent.com/pod-product-compliance
Lightning Source LLC
LaVergne TN
LVHW051818080426
835513LV00017B/2008